INTERNET PASSWORD ORGANIZER

VOL. 5

If found please contact:

Name: ___________________________

Phone: ___________________________

Email: ___________________________

Copyright: *Published in the United States by Ellie And Scott*

Published May 2018

ISBN-13: 978-1720406433
ISBN-10: 172040643X

Note

WEBSITE

DATE:	
NAME:	
USERNAME:	
PASSWORD:	
EMAIL USED:	
PHONE NUMBER:	
PIN CODE:	
SECURITY QUESTION:	
NOTES:	

WEBSITE

DATE:	
NAME:	
USERNAME:	
PASSWORD:	
EMAIL USED:	
PHONE NUMBER:	
PIN CODE:	
SECURITY QUESTION:	
NOTES:	

WEBSITE	
DATE:	
NAME:	
USERNAME:	
PASSWORD:	
EMAIL USED:	
PHONE NUMBER:	
PIN CODE:	
SECURITY QUESTION:	
NOTES:	

WEBSITE	
DATE:	
NAME:	
USERNAME:	
PASSWORD:	
EMAIL USED:	
PHONE NUMBER:	
PIN CODE:	
SECURITY QUESTION:	
NOTES:	

A

WEBSITE	
DATE:	
NAME:	
USERNAME:	
PASSWORD:	
EMAIL USED:	
PHONE NUMBER:	
PIN CODE:	
SECURITY QUESTION:	
NOTES:	

WEBSITE	
DATE:	
NAME:	
USERNAME:	
PASSWORD:	
EMAIL USED:	
PHONE NUMBER:	
PIN CODE:	
SECURITY QUESTION:	
NOTES:	

A

<table>
<tr><td>WEBSITE</td><td></td></tr>
</table>

DATE:

NAME:

USERNAME:

PASSWORD:

EMAIL USED:

PHONE NUMBER:

PIN CODE:

SECURITY QUESTION:

NOTES:

<table>
<tr><td>WEBSITE</td><td></td></tr>
</table>

DATE:

NAME:

USERNAME:

PASSWORD:

EMAIL USED:

PHONE NUMBER:

PIN CODE:

SECURITY QUESTION:

NOTES:

A

WEBSITE	
DATE:	
NAME:	
USERNAME:	
PASSWORD:	
EMAIL USED:	
PHONE NUMBER:	
PIN CODE:	
SECURITY QUESTION:	
NOTES:	

WEBSITE	
DATE:	
NAME:	
USERNAME:	
PASSWORD:	
EMAIL USED:	
PHONE NUMBER:	
PIN CODE:	
SECURITY QUESTION:	
NOTES:	

B

WEBSITE	
DATE:	
NAME:	
USERNAME:	
PASSWORD:	
EMAIL USED:	
PHONE NUMBER:	
PIN CODE:	
SECURITY QUESTION:	
NOTES:	

WEBSITE	
DATE:	
NAME:	
USERNAME:	
PASSWORD:	
EMAIL USED:	
PHONE NUMBER:	
PIN CODE:	
SECURITY QUESTION:	
NOTES:	

B

WEBSITE	
DATE:	
NAME:	
USERNAME:	
PASSWORD:	
EMAIL USED:	
PHONE NUMBER:	
PIN CODE:	
SECURITY QUESTION:	
NOTES:	

WEBSITE	
DATE:	
NAME:	
USERNAME:	
PASSWORD:	
EMAIL USED:	
PHONE NUMBER:	
PIN CODE:	
SECURITY QUESTION:	
NOTES:	

B

<table>
<tr><td>WEBSITE</td><td></td></tr>
<tr><td colspan="2">DATE:</td></tr>
<tr><td colspan="2">NAME:</td></tr>
<tr><td colspan="2">USERNAME:</td></tr>
<tr><td colspan="2">PASSWORD:</td></tr>
<tr><td colspan="2">EMAIL USED:</td></tr>
<tr><td colspan="2">PHONE NUMBER:</td></tr>
<tr><td colspan="2">PIN CODE:</td></tr>
<tr><td colspan="2">SECURITY QUESTION:</td></tr>
<tr><td colspan="2">NOTES:</td></tr>
<tr><td colspan="2"></td></tr>
<tr><td colspan="2"></td></tr>
</table>

<table>
<tr><td>WEBSITE</td><td></td></tr>
<tr><td colspan="2">DATE:</td></tr>
<tr><td colspan="2">NAME:</td></tr>
<tr><td colspan="2">USERNAME:</td></tr>
<tr><td colspan="2">PASSWORD:</td></tr>
<tr><td colspan="2">EMAIL USED:</td></tr>
<tr><td colspan="2">PHONE NUMBER:</td></tr>
<tr><td colspan="2">PIN CODE:</td></tr>
<tr><td colspan="2">SECURITY QUESTION:</td></tr>
<tr><td colspan="2">NOTES:</td></tr>
<tr><td colspan="2"></td></tr>
<tr><td colspan="2"></td></tr>
</table>

WEBSITE

DATE:

NAME:

USERNAME:

PASSWORD:

EMAIL USED:

PHONE NUMBER:

PIN CODE:

SECURITY QUESTION:

NOTES:

WEBSITE

DATE:

NAME:

USERNAME:

PASSWORD:

EMAIL USED:

PHONE NUMBER:

PIN CODE:

SECURITY QUESTION:

NOTES:

C

WEBSITE	
DATE:	
NAME:	
USERNAME:	
PASSWORD:	
EMAIL USED:	
PHONE NUMBER:	
PIN CODE:	
SECURITY QUESTION:	
NOTES:	

WEBSITE	
DATE:	
NAME:	
USERNAME:	
PASSWORD:	
EMAIL USED:	
PHONE NUMBER:	
PIN CODE:	
SECURITY QUESTION:	
NOTES:	

WEBSITE	
DATE:	
NAME:	
USERNAME:	
PASSWORD:	
EMAIL USED:	
PHONE NUMBER:	
PIN CODE:	
SECURITY QUESTION:	
NOTES:	

WEBSITE	
DATE:	
NAME:	
USERNAME:	
PASSWORD:	
EMAIL USED:	
PHONE NUMBER:	
PIN CODE:	
SECURITY QUESTION:	
NOTES:	

C

WEBSITE	
DATE:	
NAME:	
USERNAME:	
PASSWORD:	
EMAIL USED:	
PHONE NUMBER:	
PIN CODE:	
SECURITY QUESTION:	
NOTES:	

WEBSITE	
DATE:	
NAME:	
USERNAME:	
PASSWORD:	
EMAIL USED:	
PHONE NUMBER:	
PIN CODE:	
SECURITY QUESTION:	
NOTES:	

C

WEBSITE	
DATE:	
NAME:	
USERNAME:	
PASSWORD:	
EMAIL USED:	
PHONE NUMBER:	
PIN CODE:	
SECURITY QUESTION:	
NOTES:	

WEBSITE	
DATE:	
NAME:	
USERNAME:	
PASSWORD:	
EMAIL USED:	
PHONE NUMBER:	
PIN CODE:	
SECURITY QUESTION:	
NOTES:	

D

WEBSITE	
DATE:	
NAME:	
USERNAME:	
PASSWORD:	
EMAIL USED:	
PHONE NUMBER:	
PIN CODE:	
SECURITY QUESTION:	
NOTES:	

WEBSITE	
DATE:	
NAME:	
USERNAME:	
PASSWORD:	
EMAIL USED:	
PHONE NUMBER:	
PIN CODE:	
SECURITY QUESTION:	
NOTES:	

D

WEBSITE

DATE:

NAME:

USERNAME:

PASSWORD:

EMAIL USED:

PHONE NUMBER:

PIN CODE:

SECURITY QUESTION:

NOTES:

WEBSITE

DATE:

NAME:

USERNAME:

PASSWORD:

EMAIL USED:

PHONE NUMBER:

PIN CODE:

SECURITY QUESTION:

NOTES:

D

<table>
<tr><td>WEBSITE</td><td></td></tr>
</table>

DATE:
NAME:
USERNAME:
PASSWORD:
EMAIL USED:
PHONE NUMBER:
PIN CODE:
SECURITY QUESTION:
NOTES:

<table>
<tr><td>WEBSITE</td><td></td></tr>
</table>

DATE:
NAME:
USERNAME:
PASSWORD:
EMAIL USED:
PHONE NUMBER:
PIN CODE:
SECURITY QUESTION:
NOTES:

D

WEBSITE	
DATE:	
NAME:	
USERNAME:	
PASSWORD:	
EMAIL USED:	
PHONE NUMBER:	
PIN CODE:	
SECURITY QUESTION:	
NOTES:	

WEBSITE	
DATE:	
NAME:	
USERNAME:	
PASSWORD:	
EMAIL USED:	
PHONE NUMBER:	
PIN CODE:	
SECURITY QUESTION:	
NOTES:	

E

<table>
<tr><td>WEBSITE</td><td></td></tr>
</table>

DATE:
NAME:
USERNAME:
PASSWORD:
EMAIL USED:
PHONE NUMBER:
PIN CODE:
SECURITY QUESTION:
NOTES:

<table>
<tr><td>WEBSITE</td><td></td></tr>
</table>

DATE:
NAME:
USERNAME:
PASSWORD:
EMAIL USED:
PHONE NUMBER:
PIN CODE:
SECURITY QUESTION:
NOTES:

WEBSITE	
DATE:	
NAME:	
USERNAME:	
PASSWORD:	
EMAIL USED:	
PHONE NUMBER:	
PIN CODE:	
SECURITY QUESTION:	
NOTES:	

WEBSITE	
DATE:	
NAME:	
USERNAME:	
PASSWORD:	
EMAIL USED:	
PHONE NUMBER:	
PIN CODE:	
SECURITY QUESTION:	
NOTES:	

E

<table>
<tr><td>WEBSITE</td><td></td></tr>
</table>

DATE:	
NAME:	
USERNAME:	
PASSWORD:	
EMAIL USED:	
PHONE NUMBER:	
PIN CODE:	
SECURITY QUESTION:	
NOTES:	

<table>
<tr><td>WEBSITE</td><td></td></tr>
</table>

DATE:	
NAME:	
USERNAME:	
PASSWORD:	
EMAIL USED:	
PHONE NUMBER:	
PIN CODE:	
SECURITY QUESTION:	
NOTES:	

WEBSITE	
DATE:	
NAME:	
USERNAME:	
PASSWORD:	
EMAIL USED:	
PHONE NUMBER:	
PIN CODE:	
SECURITY QUESTION:	
NOTES:	

WEBSITE	
DATE:	
NAME:	
USERNAME:	
PASSWORD:	
EMAIL USED:	
PHONE NUMBER:	
PIN CODE:	
SECURITY QUESTION:	
NOTES:	

F

<table>
<tr><td>WEBSITE</td><td></td></tr>
</table>

DATE:

NAME:

USERNAME:

PASSWORD:

EMAIL USED:

PHONE NUMBER:

PIN CODE:

SECURITY QUESTION:

NOTES:

<table>
<tr><td>WEBSITE</td><td></td></tr>
</table>

DATE:

NAME:

USERNAME:

PASSWORD:

EMAIL USED:

PHONE NUMBER:

PIN CODE:

SECURITY QUESTION:

NOTES:

WEBSITE	
DATE:	
NAME:	
USERNAME:	
PASSWORD:	
EMAIL USED:	
PHONE NUMBER:	
PIN CODE:	
SECURITY QUESTION:	
NOTES:	

WEBSITE	
DATE:	
NAME:	
USERNAME:	
PASSWORD:	
EMAIL USED:	
PHONE NUMBER:	
PIN CODE:	
SECURITY QUESTION:	
NOTES:	

F

WEBSITE	
DATE:	
NAME:	
USERNAME:	
PASSWORD:	
EMAIL USED:	
PHONE NUMBER:	
PIN CODE:	
SECURITY QUESTION:	
NOTES:	

WEBSITE	
DATE:	
NAME:	
USERNAME:	
PASSWORD:	
EMAIL USED:	
PHONE NUMBER:	
PIN CODE:	
SECURITY QUESTION:	
NOTES:	

F

WEBSITE	
DATE:	
NAME:	
USERNAME:	
PASSWORD:	
EMAIL USED:	
PHONE NUMBER:	
PIN CODE:	
SECURITY QUESTION:	
NOTES:	

WEBSITE	
DATE:	
NAME:	
USERNAME:	
PASSWORD:	
EMAIL USED:	
PHONE NUMBER:	
PIN CODE:	
SECURITY QUESTION:	
NOTES:	

G

WEBSITE	
DATE:	
NAME:	
USERNAME:	
PASSWORD:	
EMAIL USED:	
PHONE NUMBER:	
PIN CODE:	
SECURITY QUESTION:	
NOTES:	

WEBSITE	
DATE:	
NAME:	
USERNAME:	
PASSWORD:	
EMAIL USED:	
PHONE NUMBER:	
PIN CODE:	
SECURITY QUESTION:	
NOTES:	

WEBSITE

DATE:

NAME:

USERNAME:

PASSWORD:

EMAIL USED:

PHONE NUMBER:

PIN CODE:

SECURITY QUESTION:

NOTES:

WEBSITE

DATE:

NAME:

USERNAME:

PASSWORD:

EMAIL USED:

PHONE NUMBER:

PIN CODE:

SECURITY QUESTION:

NOTES:

G

WEBSITE	
DATE:	
NAME:	
USERNAME:	
PASSWORD:	
EMAIL USED:	
PHONE NUMBER:	
PIN CODE:	
SECURITY QUESTION:	
NOTES:	

WEBSITE	
DATE:	
NAME:	
USERNAME:	
PASSWORD:	
EMAIL USED:	
PHONE NUMBER:	
PIN CODE:	
SECURITY QUESTION:	
NOTES:	

WEBSITE	
DATE:	
NAME:	
USERNAME:	
PASSWORD:	
EMAIL USED:	
PHONE NUMBER:	
PIN CODE:	
SECURITY QUESTION:	
NOTES:	

WEBSITE	
DATE:	
NAME:	
USERNAME:	
PASSWORD:	
EMAIL USED:	
PHONE NUMBER:	
PIN CODE:	
SECURITY QUESTION:	
NOTES:	

H

WEBSITE	
DATE:	
NAME:	
USERNAME:	
PASSWORD:	
EMAIL USED:	
PHONE NUMBER:	
PIN CODE:	
SECURITY QUESTION:	
NOTES:	

WEBSITE	
DATE:	
NAME:	
USERNAME:	
PASSWORD:	
EMAIL USED:	
PHONE NUMBER:	
PIN CODE:	
SECURITY QUESTION:	
NOTES:	

WEBSITE	
DATE:	
NAME:	
USERNAME:	
PASSWORD:	
EMAIL USED:	
PHONE NUMBER:	
PIN CODE:	
SECURITY QUESTION:	
NOTES:	

WEBSITE	
DATE:	
NAME:	
USERNAME:	
PASSWORD:	
EMAIL USED:	
PHONE NUMBER:	
PIN CODE:	
SECURITY QUESTION:	
NOTES:	

H

WEBSITE	
DATE:	
NAME:	
USERNAME:	
PASSWORD:	
EMAIL USED:	
PHONE NUMBER:	
PIN CODE:	
SECURITY QUESTION:	
NOTES:	

WEBSITE	
DATE:	
NAME:	
USERNAME:	
PASSWORD:	
EMAIL USED:	
PHONE NUMBER:	
PIN CODE:	
SECURITY QUESTION:	
NOTES:	

WEBSITE

DATE:

NAME:

USERNAME:

PASSWORD:

EMAIL USED:

PHONE NUMBER:

PIN CODE:

SECURITY QUESTION:

NOTES:

WEBSITE

DATE:

NAME:

USERNAME:

PASSWORD:

EMAIL USED:

PHONE NUMBER:

PIN CODE:

SECURITY QUESTION:

NOTES:

WEBSITE	
DATE:	
NAME:	
USERNAME:	
PASSWORD:	
EMAIL USED:	
PHONE NUMBER:	
PIN CODE:	
SECURITY QUESTION:	
NOTES:	

WEBSITE	
DATE:	
NAME:	
USERNAME:	
PASSWORD:	
EMAIL USED:	
PHONE NUMBER:	
PIN CODE:	
SECURITY QUESTION:	
NOTES:	

WEBSITE	
DATE:	
NAME:	
USERNAME:	
PASSWORD:	
EMAIL USED:	
PHONE NUMBER:	
PIN CODE:	
SECURITY QUESTION:	
NOTES:	

WEBSITE	
DATE:	
NAME:	
USERNAME:	
PASSWORD:	
EMAIL USED:	
PHONE NUMBER:	
PIN CODE:	
SECURITY QUESTION:	
NOTES:	

WEBSITE	

DATE:

NAME:

USERNAME:

PASSWORD:

EMAIL USED:

PHONE NUMBER:

PIN CODE:

SECURITY QUESTION:

NOTES:

WEBSITE	

DATE:

NAME:

USERNAME:

PASSWORD:

EMAIL USED:

PHONE NUMBER:

PIN CODE:

SECURITY QUESTION:

NOTES:

WEBSITE	
DATE:	
NAME:	
USERNAME:	
PASSWORD:	
EMAIL USED:	
PHONE NUMBER:	
PIN CODE:	
SECURITY QUESTION:	
NOTES:	

WEBSITE	
DATE:	
NAME:	
USERNAME:	
PASSWORD:	
EMAIL USED:	
PHONE NUMBER:	
PIN CODE:	
SECURITY QUESTION:	
NOTES:	

J

WEBSITE	
DATE:	
NAME:	
USERNAME:	
PASSWORD:	
EMAIL USED:	
PHONE NUMBER:	
PIN CODE:	
SECURITY QUESTION:	
NOTES:	

WEBSITE	
DATE:	
NAME:	
USERNAME:	
PASSWORD:	
EMAIL USED:	
PHONE NUMBER:	
PIN CODE:	
SECURITY QUESTION:	
NOTES:	

J

WEBSITE	
DATE:	
NAME:	
USERNAME:	
PASSWORD:	
EMAIL USED:	
PHONE NUMBER:	
PIN CODE:	
SECURITY QUESTION:	
NOTES:	

WEBSITE	
DATE:	
NAME:	
USERNAME:	
PASSWORD:	
EMAIL USED:	
PHONE NUMBER:	
PIN CODE:	
SECURITY QUESTION:	
NOTES:	

J

<table>
<tr><td>WEBSITE</td><td></td></tr>
</table>

DATE:
NAME:
USERNAME:
PASSWORD:
EMAIL USED:
PHONE NUMBER:
PIN CODE:
SECURITY QUESTION:
NOTES:

<table>
<tr><td>WEBSITE</td><td></td></tr>
</table>

DATE:
NAME:
USERNAME:
PASSWORD:
EMAIL USED:
PHONE NUMBER:
PIN CODE:
SECURITY QUESTION:
NOTES:

J

WEBSITE	
DATE:	
NAME:	
USERNAME:	
PASSWORD:	
EMAIL USED:	
PHONE NUMBER:	
PIN CODE:	
SECURITY QUESTION:	
NOTES:	

WEBSITE	
DATE:	
NAME:	
USERNAME:	
PASSWORD:	
EMAIL USED:	
PHONE NUMBER:	
PIN CODE:	
SECURITY QUESTION:	
NOTES:	

K

WEBSITE	
DATE:	
NAME:	
USERNAME:	
PASSWORD:	
EMAIL USED:	
PHONE NUMBER:	
PIN CODE:	
SECURITY QUESTION:	
NOTES:	

WEBSITE	
DATE:	
NAME:	
USERNAME:	
PASSWORD:	
EMAIL USED:	
PHONE NUMBER:	
PIN CODE:	
SECURITY QUESTION:	
NOTES:	

K

WEBSITE	
DATE:	
NAME:	
USERNAME:	
PASSWORD:	
EMAIL USED:	
PHONE NUMBER:	
PIN CODE:	
SECURITY QUESTION:	
NOTES:	

WEBSITE	
DATE:	
NAME:	
USERNAME:	
PASSWORD:	
EMAIL USED:	
PHONE NUMBER:	
PIN CODE:	
SECURITY QUESTION:	
NOTES:	

K

WEBSITE	
DATE:	
NAME:	
USERNAME:	
PASSWORD:	
EMAIL USED:	
PHONE NUMBER:	
PIN CODE:	
SECURITY QUESTION:	
NOTES:	

WEBSITE	
DATE:	
NAME:	
USERNAME:	
PASSWORD:	
EMAIL USED:	
PHONE NUMBER:	
PIN CODE:	
SECURITY QUESTION:	
NOTES:	

WEBSITE

DATE:	
NAME:	
USERNAME:	
PASSWORD:	
EMAIL USED:	
PHONE NUMBER:	
PIN CODE:	
SECURITY QUESTION:	
NOTES:	

WEBSITE

DATE:	
NAME:	
USERNAME:	
PASSWORD:	
EMAIL USED:	
PHONE NUMBER:	
PIN CODE:	
SECURITY QUESTION:	
NOTES:	

L

WEBSITE	
DATE:	
NAME:	
USERNAME:	
PASSWORD:	
EMAIL USED:	
PHONE NUMBER:	
PIN CODE:	
SECURITY QUESTION:	
NOTES:	

WEBSITE	
DATE:	
NAME:	
USERNAME:	
PASSWORD:	
EMAIL USED:	
PHONE NUMBER:	
PIN CODE:	
SECURITY QUESTION:	
NOTES:	

WEBSITE

DATE:

NAME:

USERNAME:

PASSWORD:

EMAIL USED:

PHONE NUMBER:

PIN CODE:

SECURITY QUESTION:

NOTES:

WEBSITE

DATE:

NAME:

USERNAME:

PASSWORD:

EMAIL USED:

PHONE NUMBER:

PIN CODE:

SECURITY QUESTION:

NOTES:

L

<table>
<tr><td>WEBSITE</td><td></td></tr>
<tr><td>DATE:</td></tr>
<tr><td>NAME:</td></tr>
<tr><td>USERNAME:</td></tr>
<tr><td>PASSWORD:</td></tr>
<tr><td>EMAIL USED:</td></tr>
<tr><td>PHONE NUMBER:</td></tr>
<tr><td>PIN CODE:</td></tr>
<tr><td>SECURITY QUESTION:</td></tr>
<tr><td>NOTES:</td></tr>
<tr><td></td></tr>
<tr><td></td></tr>
</table>

<table>
<tr><td>WEBSITE</td><td></td></tr>
<tr><td>DATE:</td></tr>
<tr><td>NAME:</td></tr>
<tr><td>USERNAME:</td></tr>
<tr><td>PASSWORD:</td></tr>
<tr><td>EMAIL USED:</td></tr>
<tr><td>PHONE NUMBER:</td></tr>
<tr><td>PIN CODE:</td></tr>
<tr><td>SECURITY QUESTION:</td></tr>
<tr><td>NOTES:</td></tr>
<tr><td></td></tr>
<tr><td></td></tr>
</table>

L

WEBSITE	
DATE:	
NAME:	
USERNAME:	
PASSWORD:	
EMAIL USED:	
PHONE NUMBER:	
PIN CODE:	
SECURITY QUESTION:	
NOTES:	

WEBSITE	
DATE:	
NAME:	
USERNAME:	
PASSWORD:	
EMAIL USED:	
PHONE NUMBER:	
PIN CODE:	
SECURITY QUESTION:	
NOTES:	

M

WEBSITE	
DATE:	
NAME:	
USERNAME:	
PASSWORD:	
EMAIL USED:	
PHONE NUMBER:	
PIN CODE:	
SECURITY QUESTION:	
NOTES:	

WEBSITE	
DATE:	
NAME:	
USERNAME:	
PASSWORD:	
EMAIL USED:	
PHONE NUMBER:	
PIN CODE:	
SECURITY QUESTION:	
NOTES:	

WEBSITE	
DATE:	
NAME:	
USERNAME:	
PASSWORD:	
EMAIL USED:	
PHONE NUMBER:	
PIN CODE:	
SECURITY QUESTION:	
NOTES:	

WEBSITE	
DATE:	
NAME:	
USERNAME:	
PASSWORD:	
EMAIL USED:	
PHONE NUMBER:	
PIN CODE:	
SECURITY QUESTION:	
NOTES:	

WEBSITE

DATE:	
NAME:	
USERNAME:	
PASSWORD:	
EMAIL USED:	
PHONE NUMBER:	
PIN CODE:	
SECURITY QUESTION:	
NOTES:	

WEBSITE

DATE:	
NAME:	
USERNAME:	
PASSWORD:	
EMAIL USED:	
PHONE NUMBER:	
PIN CODE:	
SECURITY QUESTION:	
NOTES:	

WEBSITE	
DATE:	
NAME:	
USERNAME:	
PASSWORD:	
EMAIL USED:	
PHONE NUMBER:	
PIN CODE:	
SECURITY QUESTION:	
NOTES:	

WEBSITE	
DATE:	
NAME:	
USERNAME:	
PASSWORD:	
EMAIL USED:	
PHONE NUMBER:	
PIN CODE:	
SECURITY QUESTION:	
NOTES:	

N

WEBSITE	
DATE:	
NAME:	
USERNAME:	
PASSWORD:	
EMAIL USED:	
PHONE NUMBER:	
PIN CODE:	
SECURITY QUESTION:	
NOTES:	

WEBSITE	
DATE:	
NAME:	
USERNAME:	
PASSWORD:	
EMAIL USED:	
PHONE NUMBER:	
PIN CODE:	
SECURITY QUESTION:	
NOTES:	

WEBSITE	
DATE:	
NAME:	
USERNAME:	
PASSWORD:	
EMAIL USED:	
PHONE NUMBER:	
PIN CODE:	
SECURITY QUESTION:	
NOTES:	

WEBSITE	
DATE:	
NAME:	
USERNAME:	
PASSWORD:	
EMAIL USED:	
PHONE NUMBER:	
PIN CODE:	
SECURITY QUESTION:	
NOTES:	

N

WEBSITE	
DATE:	
NAME:	
USERNAME:	
PASSWORD:	
EMAIL USED:	
PHONE NUMBER:	
PIN CODE:	
SECURITY QUESTION:	
NOTES:	

WEBSITE	
DATE:	
NAME:	
USERNAME:	
PASSWORD:	
EMAIL USED:	
PHONE NUMBER:	
PIN CODE:	
SECURITY QUESTION:	
NOTES:	

WEBSITE

DATE:

NAME:

USERNAME:

PASSWORD:

EMAIL USED:

PHONE NUMBER:

PIN CODE:

SECURITY QUESTION:

NOTES:

WEBSITE

DATE:

NAME:

USERNAME:

PASSWORD:

EMAIL USED:

PHONE NUMBER:

PIN CODE:

SECURITY QUESTION:

NOTES:

WEBSITE

DATE:	
NAME:	
USERNAME:	
PASSWORD:	
EMAIL USED:	
PHONE NUMBER:	
PIN CODE:	
SECURITY QUESTION:	
NOTES:	

WEBSITE

DATE:	
NAME:	
USERNAME:	
PASSWORD:	
EMAIL USED:	
PHONE NUMBER:	
PIN CODE:	
SECURITY QUESTION:	
NOTES:	

WEBSITE	

DATE:

NAME:

USERNAME:

PASSWORD:

EMAIL USED:

PHONE NUMBER:

PIN CODE:

SECURITY QUESTION:

NOTES:

WEBSITE	

DATE:

NAME:

USERNAME:

PASSWORD:

EMAIL USED:

PHONE NUMBER:

PIN CODE:

SECURITY QUESTION:

NOTES:

WEBSITE

DATE:	
NAME:	
USERNAME:	
PASSWORD:	
EMAIL USED:	
PHONE NUMBER:	
PIN CODE:	
SECURITY QUESTION:	
NOTES:	

WEBSITE

DATE:	
NAME:	
USERNAME:	
PASSWORD:	
EMAIL USED:	
PHONE NUMBER:	
PIN CODE:	
SECURITY QUESTION:	
NOTES:	

<table>
<tr><td>WEBSITE</td><td></td></tr>
</table>

| DATE: |
| NAME: |
| USERNAME: |
| PASSWORD: |
| EMAIL USED: |
| PHONE NUMBER: |
| PIN CODE: |
| SECURITY QUESTION: |
| NOTES: |
| |
| |

<table>
<tr><td>WEBSITE</td><td></td></tr>
</table>

| DATE: |
| NAME: |
| USERNAME: |
| PASSWORD: |
| EMAIL USED: |
| PHONE NUMBER: |
| PIN CODE: |
| SECURITY QUESTION: |
| NOTES: |
| |
| |

P

WEBSITE	
DATE:	
NAME:	
USERNAME:	
PASSWORD:	
EMAIL USED:	
PHONE NUMBER:	
PIN CODE:	
SECURITY QUESTION:	
NOTES:	

WEBSITE	
DATE:	
NAME:	
USERNAME:	
PASSWORD:	
EMAIL USED:	
PHONE NUMBER:	
PIN CODE:	
SECURITY QUESTION:	
NOTES:	

WEBSITE	
DATE:	
NAME:	
USERNAME:	
PASSWORD:	
EMAIL USED:	
PHONE NUMBER:	
PIN CODE:	
SECURITY QUESTION:	
NOTES:	

WEBSITE	
DATE:	
NAME:	
USERNAME:	
PASSWORD:	
EMAIL USED:	
PHONE NUMBER:	
PIN CODE:	
SECURITY QUESTION:	
NOTES:	

P

WEBSITE

DATE:

NAME:

USERNAME:

PASSWORD:

EMAIL USED:

PHONE NUMBER:

PIN CODE:

SECURITY QUESTION:

NOTES:

WEBSITE

DATE:

NAME:

USERNAME:

PASSWORD:

EMAIL USED:

PHONE NUMBER:

PIN CODE:

SECURITY QUESTION:

NOTES:

P

WEBSITE	

DATE:

NAME:

USERNAME:

PASSWORD:

EMAIL USED:

PHONE NUMBER:

PIN CODE:

SECURITY QUESTION:

NOTES:

WEBSITE	

DATE:

NAME:

USERNAME:

PASSWORD:

EMAIL USED:

PHONE NUMBER:

PIN CODE:

SECURITY QUESTION:

NOTES:

Q

WEBSITE	
DATE:	
NAME:	
USERNAME:	
PASSWORD:	
EMAIL USED:	
PHONE NUMBER:	
PIN CODE:	
SECURITY QUESTION:	
NOTES:	

WEBSITE	
DATE:	
NAME:	
USERNAME:	
PASSWORD:	
EMAIL USED:	
PHONE NUMBER:	
PIN CODE:	
SECURITY QUESTION:	
NOTES:	

Q

WEBSITE

DATE:

NAME:

USERNAME:

PASSWORD:

EMAIL USED:

PHONE NUMBER:

PIN CODE:

SECURITY QUESTION:

NOTES:

WEBSITE

DATE:

NAME:

USERNAME:

PASSWORD:

EMAIL USED:

PHONE NUMBER:

PIN CODE:

SECURITY QUESTION:

NOTES:

Q

WEBSITE	
DATE:	
NAME:	
USERNAME:	
PASSWORD:	
EMAIL USED:	
PHONE NUMBER:	
PIN CODE:	
SECURITY QUESTION:	
NOTES:	

WEBSITE	
DATE:	
NAME:	
USERNAME:	
PASSWORD:	
EMAIL USED:	
PHONE NUMBER:	
PIN CODE:	
SECURITY QUESTION:	
NOTES:	

WEBSITE	
DATE:	
NAME:	
USERNAME:	
PASSWORD:	
EMAIL USED:	
PHONE NUMBER:	
PIN CODE:	
SECURITY QUESTION:	
NOTES:	

WEBSITE	
DATE:	
NAME:	
USERNAME:	
PASSWORD:	
EMAIL USED:	
PHONE NUMBER:	
PIN CODE:	
SECURITY QUESTION:	
NOTES:	

R

WEBSITE	
DATE:	
NAME:	
USERNAME:	
PASSWORD:	
EMAIL USED:	
PHONE NUMBER:	
PIN CODE:	
SECURITY QUESTION:	
NOTES:	

WEBSITE	
DATE:	
NAME:	
USERNAME:	
PASSWORD:	
EMAIL USED:	
PHONE NUMBER:	
PIN CODE:	
SECURITY QUESTION:	
NOTES:	

WEBSITE	
DATE:	
NAME:	
USERNAME:	
PASSWORD:	
EMAIL USED:	
PHONE NUMBER:	
PIN CODE:	
SECURITY QUESTION:	
NOTES:	

WEBSITE	
DATE:	
NAME:	
USERNAME:	
PASSWORD:	
EMAIL USED:	
PHONE NUMBER:	
PIN CODE:	
SECURITY QUESTION:	
NOTES:	

R

<table>
<tr><td>WEBSITE</td><td></td></tr>
</table>

DATE:

NAME:

USERNAME:

PASSWORD:

EMAIL USED:

PHONE NUMBER:

PIN CODE:

SECURITY QUESTION:

NOTES:

<table>
<tr><td>WEBSITE</td><td></td></tr>
</table>

DATE:

NAME:

USERNAME:

PASSWORD:

EMAIL USED:

PHONE NUMBER:

PIN CODE:

SECURITY QUESTION:

NOTES:

R

WEBSITE	
DATE:	
NAME:	
USERNAME:	
PASSWORD:	
EMAIL USED:	
PHONE NUMBER:	
PIN CODE:	
SECURITY QUESTION:	
NOTES:	

WEBSITE	
DATE:	
NAME:	
USERNAME:	
PASSWORD:	
EMAIL USED:	
PHONE NUMBER:	
PIN CODE:	
SECURITY QUESTION:	
NOTES:	

S

<table>
<tr><td>WEBSITE</td><td></td></tr>
</table>

DATE:

NAME:

USERNAME:

PASSWORD:

EMAIL USED:

PHONE NUMBER:

PIN CODE:

SECURITY QUESTION:

NOTES:

<table>
<tr><td>WEBSITE</td><td></td></tr>
</table>

DATE:

NAME:

USERNAME:

PASSWORD:

EMAIL USED:

PHONE NUMBER:

PIN CODE:

SECURITY QUESTION:

NOTES:

WEBSITE	
DATE:	
NAME:	
USERNAME:	
PASSWORD:	
EMAIL USED:	
PHONE NUMBER:	
PIN CODE:	
SECURITY QUESTION:	
NOTES:	

WEBSITE	
DATE:	
NAME:	
USERNAME:	
PASSWORD:	
EMAIL USED:	
PHONE NUMBER:	
PIN CODE:	
SECURITY QUESTION:	
NOTES:	

S

WEBSITE	
DATE:	
NAME:	
USERNAME:	
PASSWORD:	
EMAIL USED:	
PHONE NUMBER:	
PIN CODE:	
SECURITY QUESTION:	
NOTES:	

WEBSITE	
DATE:	
NAME:	
USERNAME:	
PASSWORD:	
EMAIL USED:	
PHONE NUMBER:	
PIN CODE:	
SECURITY QUESTION:	
NOTES:	

WEBSITE	
DATE:	
NAME:	
USERNAME:	
PASSWORD:	
EMAIL USED:	
PHONE NUMBER:	
PIN CODE:	
SECURITY QUESTION:	
NOTES:	

WEBSITE	
DATE:	
NAME:	
USERNAME:	
PASSWORD:	
EMAIL USED:	
PHONE NUMBER:	
PIN CODE:	
SECURITY QUESTION:	
NOTES:	

<table>
<tr><td colspan="2">WEBSITE</td></tr>
<tr><td>DATE:</td><td></td></tr>
<tr><td>NAME:</td><td></td></tr>
<tr><td>USERNAME:</td><td></td></tr>
<tr><td>PASSWORD:</td><td></td></tr>
<tr><td>EMAIL USED:</td><td></td></tr>
<tr><td>PHONE NUMBER:</td><td></td></tr>
<tr><td>PIN CODE:</td><td></td></tr>
<tr><td>SECURITY QUESTION:</td><td></td></tr>
<tr><td>NOTES:</td><td></td></tr>
<tr><td></td><td></td></tr>
<tr><td></td><td></td></tr>
</table>

<table>
<tr><td colspan="2">WEBSITE</td></tr>
<tr><td>DATE:</td><td></td></tr>
<tr><td>NAME:</td><td></td></tr>
<tr><td>USERNAME:</td><td></td></tr>
<tr><td>PASSWORD:</td><td></td></tr>
<tr><td>EMAIL USED:</td><td></td></tr>
<tr><td>PHONE NUMBER:</td><td></td></tr>
<tr><td>PIN CODE:</td><td></td></tr>
<tr><td>SECURITY QUESTION:</td><td></td></tr>
<tr><td>NOTES:</td><td></td></tr>
<tr><td></td><td></td></tr>
<tr><td></td><td></td></tr>
</table>

T

WEBSITE	
DATE:	
NAME:	
USERNAME:	
PASSWORD:	
EMAIL USED:	
PHONE NUMBER:	
PIN CODE:	
SECURITY QUESTION:	
NOTES:	

WEBSITE	
DATE:	
NAME:	
USERNAME:	
PASSWORD:	
EMAIL USED:	
PHONE NUMBER:	
PIN CODE:	
SECURITY QUESTION:	
NOTES:	

<table>
<tr><td>WEBSITE</td><td></td></tr>
</table>

| DATE: |
| NAME: |
| USERNAME: |
| PASSWORD: |
| EMAIL USED: |
| PHONE NUMBER: |
| PIN CODE: |
| SECURITY QUESTION: |
| NOTES: |
| |
| |

<table>
<tr><td>WEBSITE</td><td></td></tr>
</table>

| DATE: |
| NAME: |
| USERNAME: |
| PASSWORD: |
| EMAIL USED: |
| PHONE NUMBER: |
| PIN CODE: |
| SECURITY QUESTION: |
| NOTES: |
| |
| |

T

WEBSITE	
DATE:	
NAME:	
USERNAME:	
PASSWORD:	
EMAIL USED:	
PHONE NUMBER:	
PIN CODE:	
SECURITY QUESTION:	
NOTES:	

WEBSITE	
DATE:	
NAME:	
USERNAME:	
PASSWORD:	
EMAIL USED:	
PHONE NUMBER:	
PIN CODE:	
SECURITY QUESTION:	
NOTES:	

U

<table>
<tr><td>WEBSITE</td><td></td></tr>
</table>

DATE:

NAME:

USERNAME:

PASSWORD:

EMAIL USED:

PHONE NUMBER:

PIN CODE:

SECURITY QUESTION:

NOTES:

<table>
<tr><td>WEBSITE</td><td></td></tr>
</table>

DATE:

NAME:

USERNAME:

PASSWORD:

EMAIL USED:

PHONE NUMBER:

PIN CODE:

SECURITY QUESTION:

NOTES:

WEBSITE	
DATE:	
NAME:	
USERNAME:	
PASSWORD:	
EMAIL USED:	
PHONE NUMBER:	
PIN CODE:	
SECURITY QUESTION:	
NOTES:	

WEBSITE	
DATE:	
NAME:	
USERNAME:	
PASSWORD:	
EMAIL USED:	
PHONE NUMBER:	
PIN CODE:	
SECURITY QUESTION:	
NOTES:	

U

WEBSITE	
DATE:	
NAME:	
USERNAME:	
PASSWORD:	
EMAIL USED:	
PHONE NUMBER:	
PIN CODE:	
SECURITY QUESTION:	
NOTES:	

WEBSITE	
DATE:	
NAME:	
USERNAME:	
PASSWORD:	
EMAIL USED:	
PHONE NUMBER:	
PIN CODE:	
SECURITY QUESTION:	
NOTES:	

WEBSITE	
DATE:	
NAME:	
USERNAME:	
PASSWORD:	
EMAIL USED:	
PHONE NUMBER:	
PIN CODE:	
SECURITY QUESTION:	
NOTES:	

WEBSITE	
DATE:	
NAME:	
USERNAME:	
PASSWORD:	
EMAIL USED:	
PHONE NUMBER:	
PIN CODE:	
SECURITY QUESTION:	
NOTES:	

V

WEBSITE	
DATE:	
NAME:	
USERNAME:	
PASSWORD:	
EMAIL USED:	
PHONE NUMBER:	
PIN CODE:	
SECURITY QUESTION:	
NOTES:	

WEBSITE	
DATE:	
NAME:	
USERNAME:	
PASSWORD:	
EMAIL USED:	
PHONE NUMBER:	
PIN CODE:	
SECURITY QUESTION:	
NOTES:	

<table>
<tr><td colspan="2">WEBSITE</td></tr>
<tr><td>DATE:</td><td></td></tr>
<tr><td>NAME:</td><td></td></tr>
<tr><td>USERNAME:</td><td></td></tr>
<tr><td>PASSWORD:</td><td></td></tr>
<tr><td>EMAIL USED:</td><td></td></tr>
<tr><td>PHONE NUMBER:</td><td></td></tr>
<tr><td>PIN CODE:</td><td></td></tr>
<tr><td>SECURITY QUESTION:</td><td></td></tr>
<tr><td>NOTES:</td><td></td></tr>
<tr><td></td><td></td></tr>
<tr><td></td><td></td></tr>
</table>

<table>
<tr><td colspan="2">WEBSITE</td></tr>
<tr><td>DATE:</td><td></td></tr>
<tr><td>NAME:</td><td></td></tr>
<tr><td>USERNAME:</td><td></td></tr>
<tr><td>PASSWORD:</td><td></td></tr>
<tr><td>EMAIL USED:</td><td></td></tr>
<tr><td>PHONE NUMBER:</td><td></td></tr>
<tr><td>PIN CODE:</td><td></td></tr>
<tr><td>SECURITY QUESTION:</td><td></td></tr>
<tr><td>NOTES:</td><td></td></tr>
<tr><td></td><td></td></tr>
<tr><td></td><td></td></tr>
</table>

V

WEBSITE	
DATE:	
NAME:	
USERNAME:	
PASSWORD:	
EMAIL USED:	
PHONE NUMBER:	
PIN CODE:	
SECURITY QUESTION:	
NOTES:	

WEBSITE	
DATE:	
NAME:	
USERNAME:	
PASSWORD:	
EMAIL USED:	
PHONE NUMBER:	
PIN CODE:	
SECURITY QUESTION:	
NOTES:	

V

WEBSITE	
DATE:	
NAME:	
USERNAME:	
PASSWORD:	
EMAIL USED:	
PHONE NUMBER:	
PIN CODE:	
SECURITY QUESTION:	
NOTES:	

WEBSITE	
DATE:	
NAME:	
USERNAME:	
PASSWORD:	
EMAIL USED:	
PHONE NUMBER:	
PIN CODE:	
SECURITY QUESTION:	
NOTES:	

WEBSITE

DATE:	
NAME:	
USERNAME:	
PASSWORD:	
EMAIL USED:	
PHONE NUMBER:	
PIN CODE:	
SECURITY QUESTION:	
NOTES:	

WEBSITE

DATE:	
NAME:	
USERNAME:	
PASSWORD:	
EMAIL USED:	
PHONE NUMBER:	
PIN CODE:	
SECURITY QUESTION:	
NOTES:	

W

WEBSITE	

DATE:

NAME:

USERNAME:

PASSWORD:

EMAIL USED:

PHONE NUMBER:

PIN CODE:

SECURITY QUESTION:

NOTES:

WEBSITE	

DATE:

NAME:

USERNAME:

PASSWORD:

EMAIL USED:

PHONE NUMBER:

PIN CODE:

SECURITY QUESTION:

NOTES:

WEBSITE	
DATE:	
NAME:	
USERNAME:	
PASSWORD:	
EMAIL USED:	
PHONE NUMBER:	
PIN CODE:	
SECURITY QUESTION:	
NOTES:	

WEBSITE	
DATE:	
NAME:	
USERNAME:	
PASSWORD:	
EMAIL USED:	
PHONE NUMBER:	
PIN CODE:	
SECURITY QUESTION:	
NOTES:	

WEBSITE	
DATE:	
NAME:	
USERNAME:	
PASSWORD:	
EMAIL USED:	
PHONE NUMBER:	
PIN CODE:	
SECURITY QUESTION:	
NOTES:	

WEBSITE	
DATE:	
NAME:	
USERNAME:	
PASSWORD:	
EMAIL USED:	
PHONE NUMBER:	
PIN CODE:	
SECURITY QUESTION:	
NOTES:	

X

WEBSITE	
DATE:	
NAME:	
USERNAME:	
PASSWORD:	
EMAIL USED:	
PHONE NUMBER:	
PIN CODE:	
SECURITY QUESTION:	
NOTES:	

WEBSITE	
DATE:	
NAME:	
USERNAME:	
PASSWORD:	
EMAIL USED:	
PHONE NUMBER:	
PIN CODE:	
SECURITY QUESTION:	
NOTES:	

X

WEBSITE	
DATE:	
NAME:	
USERNAME:	
PASSWORD:	
EMAIL USED:	
PHONE NUMBER:	
PIN CODE:	
SECURITY QUESTION:	
NOTES:	

WEBSITE	
DATE:	
NAME:	
USERNAME:	
PASSWORD:	
EMAIL USED:	
PHONE NUMBER:	
PIN CODE:	
SECURITY QUESTION:	
NOTES:	

WEBSITE	
DATE:	
NAME:	
USERNAME:	
PASSWORD:	
EMAIL USED:	
PHONE NUMBER:	
PIN CODE:	
SECURITY QUESTION:	
NOTES:	

WEBSITE	
DATE:	
NAME:	
USERNAME:	
PASSWORD:	
EMAIL USED:	
PHONE NUMBER:	
PIN CODE:	
SECURITY QUESTION:	
NOTES:	

X

WEBSITE	
DATE:	
NAME:	
USERNAME:	
PASSWORD:	
EMAIL USED:	
PHONE NUMBER:	
PIN CODE:	
SECURITY QUESTION:	
NOTES:	

WEBSITE	
DATE:	
NAME:	
USERNAME:	
PASSWORD:	
EMAIL USED:	
PHONE NUMBER:	
PIN CODE:	
SECURITY QUESTION:	
NOTES:	

Y

<table>
<tr><td>**WEBSITE**</td><td></td></tr>
</table>

| DATE: |
| NAME: |
| USERNAME: |
| PASSWORD: |
| EMAIL USED: |
| PHONE NUMBER: |
| PIN CODE: |
| SECURITY QUESTION: |
| NOTES: |
| |
| |

<table>
<tr><td>**WEBSITE**</td><td></td></tr>
</table>

| DATE: |
| NAME: |
| USERNAME: |
| PASSWORD: |
| EMAIL USED: |
| PHONE NUMBER: |
| PIN CODE: |
| SECURITY QUESTION: |
| NOTES: |
| |
| |

WEBSITE

DATE:

NAME:

USERNAME:

PASSWORD:

EMAIL USED:

PHONE NUMBER:

PIN CODE:

SECURITY QUESTION:

NOTES:

WEBSITE

DATE:

NAME:

USERNAME:

PASSWORD:

EMAIL USED:

PHONE NUMBER:

PIN CODE:

SECURITY QUESTION:

NOTES:

Y

WEBSITE	
DATE:	
NAME:	
USERNAME:	
PASSWORD:	
EMAIL USED:	
PHONE NUMBER:	
PIN CODE:	
SECURITY QUESTION:	
NOTES:	

WEBSITE	
DATE:	
NAME:	
USERNAME:	
PASSWORD:	
EMAIL USED:	
PHONE NUMBER:	
PIN CODE:	
SECURITY QUESTION:	
NOTES:	

WEBSITE	
DATE:	
NAME:	
USERNAME:	
PASSWORD:	
EMAIL USED:	
PHONE NUMBER:	
PIN CODE:	
SECURITY QUESTION:	
NOTES:	

WEBSITE	
DATE:	
NAME:	
USERNAME:	
PASSWORD:	
EMAIL USED:	
PHONE NUMBER:	
PIN CODE:	
SECURITY QUESTION:	
NOTES:	

Z

WEBSITE	
DATE:	
NAME:	
USERNAME:	
PASSWORD:	
EMAIL USED:	
PHONE NUMBER:	
PIN CODE:	
SECURITY QUESTION:	
NOTES:	

WEBSITE	
DATE:	
NAME:	
USERNAME:	
PASSWORD:	
EMAIL USED:	
PHONE NUMBER:	
PIN CODE:	
SECURITY QUESTION:	
NOTES:	

WEBSITE	
DATE:	
NAME:	
USERNAME:	
PASSWORD:	
EMAIL USED:	
PHONE NUMBER:	
PIN CODE:	
SECURITY QUESTION:	
NOTES:	

WEBSITE	
DATE:	
NAME:	
USERNAME:	
PASSWORD:	
EMAIL USED:	
PHONE NUMBER:	
PIN CODE:	
SECURITY QUESTION:	
NOTES:	

Z

<table>
<tr><td>WEBSITE</td><td></td></tr>
</table>

DATE:

NAME:

USERNAME:

PASSWORD:

EMAIL USED:

PHONE NUMBER:

PIN CODE:

SECURITY QUESTION:

NOTES:

<table>
<tr><td>WEBSITE</td><td></td></tr>
</table>

DATE:

NAME:

USERNAME:

PASSWORD:

EMAIL USED:

PHONE NUMBER:

PIN CODE:

SECURITY QUESTION:

NOTES:

WEBSITE

DATE:

NAME:

USERNAME:

PASSWORD:

EMAIL USED:

PHONE NUMBER:

PIN CODE:

SECURITY QUESTION:

NOTES:

WEBSITE

DATE:

NAME:

USERNAME:

PASSWORD:

EMAIL USED:

PHONE NUMBER:

PIN CODE:

SECURITY QUESTION:

NOTES:

<table>
<tr><td>WEBSITE</td><td></td></tr>
</table>

DATE:

NAME:

USERNAME:

PASSWORD:

EMAIL USED:

PHONE NUMBER:

PIN CODE:

SECURITY QUESTION:

NOTES:

<table>
<tr><td>WEBSITE</td><td></td></tr>
</table>

DATE:

NAME:

USERNAME:

PASSWORD:

EMAIL USED:

PHONE NUMBER:

PIN CODE:

SECURITY QUESTION:

NOTES:

Note

Made in the USA
Monee, IL
07 July 2026

56551659R00066